Emotional Fluctuations

(And Other Stories)

Stéphanie Bouchard

Emotional Fluctuations (And Other Stories)
Copyright © 2023 by Stéphanie Bouchard

All rights reserved. No part of this publication may be reproduced, distributed, or transmitted in any form or by any means, including photocopying, recording, or other electronic or mechanical methods, without the prior written permission of the author, except in the case of brief quotations embodied in critical reviews and certain other non-commercial uses permitted by copyright law.

Tellwell Talent
www.tellwell.ca

ISBN
978-0-2288-9273-1 (Paperback)
978-0-2288-9274-8 (eBook)

The Rain

The rain does not apologize
for making you soaking wet.
It pours down strong
and soaks the ground,
with no worries or regrets.

A Vision in Silver Sequence

She is a vision in silver sequence
with lips of red so fine,
with dangling earrings of sapphire;
a tall glass filled with wine.

Gaze upon those heavenly blues;
her beauty is sublime.
They swing back and forth
like a pendulum,
with a round-cut diamond's shine.

I wonder what hides behind
those tresses, that smile, those eyes?
I cross my heart and hope to die,
that I have found my soulmate tonight.

Dark Depths

Empty are the souls of the fallen.
In dark depths they shall rejoice,
there where light is dim
and regrets are at their finest.

Into Pieces

Cut my skin off into pieces.
Let it bleed and touch the ground,
for it does not make me feel good—
it does not belong.
The skin weighs too heavily
on my body and my spine.
Its excess is a burden
that weighs heavily on my mind.
It stresses me so—
I need to let things go.
In acceptance, I will find
it takes time to heal and bind.

Personalities

Sometimes, personalities,
they do not click.
They do not match.
Do not try to fit two pieces
that were never meant to latch,
for they will definitely clash.

Vision of Innocence

A vision of innocence,
framed still in an instance.
Her potential will surpass the odds,
for she is a princess
in her pale white dress.
I appreciate all her wonders
and sob.

La mère berce

Les vagues frappent
le bord du sable constamment
ici vue, la berceuse de l'océan
comme la mer
si tendre et calmement
la mère berce
et endort son enfant

The Heart

The first thing that stopped was the heart.
First, there was the deep pain.
Then, in time, everything stopped.
There was no pain—she lay in bed
with just the images of her life
passing through her head.

Little Birdie

I'm sorry little birdie,
that you didn't get the chance to fly,
to feel the breeze under your wings,
in the sunny northern sky.

Broken Glass

Broken glass fills the floor
with sharp, vicious fragments.
It extends over the space
with intents of pain, by sharpness.

Fog Beneath the Trees

Fog beneath the trees,
a mystic scenery.
The heavy, dark grey skies
make wide, a sleepy eye.
The sky has turned to dark,
tearing the brittle bark;
the rain, a refreshing shower
comes rushing in for the flowers.
Makes them grow fast and tall,
above the foggy mess of it all.

Heartbeats

This is where I find comfort,
when we are apart.
I can find you, where the beats won't stop—
in the middle of my heart.

Untold Stories

In the deepest depths of my soul
lie the stories that are untold.
They are locked up in a vault.
Words are stuck; I cannot talk.
Memories linger from a distance,
not even sure of their existence.
Was it real or was it not?
Let's go forth in useless thought—
my memories are all I've got.
So, let them be of merry days
and positive thoughts
that lead to joyous days,
with golden kisses from
the sun's glorious rays.

Slippery Slope

Your life
is like trying to climb
a slope so muddy,
every time you take a step up,
you fall three down
because it is so slippery.

Lullaby

Sing me a song blue bird,
high in the sky.
No one can touch you,
my lullaby.

Infuriate Me

Infuriate me; make me mad.
Insult me; make me sad.
Twist my words,
invent stories—
depression is a sore body.
Talk of me, behind my back.
Please, tell lies to make me crack.

Maman! viens courir avec moi

Maman! Viens courir avec moi
en cette journée ensoleillée
viens regarder les nuages
ils se transforment en idées

ils deviennent des formes
et des bonhommes
c'est tellement rigolo

viens voir les insectes
ils sautent très haut
c'est un des jours
les plus beaux

cours avec moi pieds nus
l'herbe chatouille mes petits orteils
regarde la fleur
elle accueille cette abeille

je t'aime, tu es mon idole
regarde comme l'oiseau vole
très haut dans le ciel bleu
la couleur de tes yeux

maman! pousse-moi sur la balançoire

je veux aller très vite
veux-tu m'entendre chanter
à haute voix?
maman . . . viens courir avec moi!

Follow Me

Follow me onto this pebbled path …
There, something great awaits.
Let your feet glide across the wet of night,
in a cold and dark embrace

Follow me to the place …
where the stars and moon align
in the dark and empty fields.
Where fresh air comes, easy to find.

The Lady With the Fancy Hat...

The problems were the same, no matter where you'd go;
the lady with the fancy hat had to put on a show.
The shy housewife sat around and kept quietly to herself;
the other had lots of money, way too much for oneself.
She went through it like water, while the housewives lived in stress;
being labelled a drama queen fitted her the best.
While the lady in the hat, so tall, proceeded to make the others feel small,
the housewife stood up and opened wide, in hopes to make a change:
"I might not have lots of money, but indeed I have my pride!
To laugh at some and to bring down others, just isn't my style.
Money comes and goes, but personality is for life.
I'm sorry to say that your soul is, indeed, as black as night."

The In-Betweens

Everything's falling into place.
At night, it all comes to life.
I am screening for the in-betweens,
the things that are unseen.
These shadows on the wall,
are (to my surprise) when I fall,
the dark, unknown shapes
that seem to crawl.

Into the Snow

And into the snow I go,
to catch a chill,
find my thrill,
and regain my
will to live.

Entwined

A thousand tears have fallen on your shoulder—
they have been only mine.
Many nights of tears and laughter—
minds and feelings, entwined.

If I Fall

I'm sitting on the edge.
What happens if I fall?
I won't remember anything,
anything at all.
All the things I've felt,
all the memories in my head,
I won't recall.
I won't feel anything,
nothing at all.
I choose to fall for life
and every adventure that comes with it.
To life, I will commit.
I will fall but never quit.

Divided

This road that divides the
grass and the rocks
divides the pieces
that aren't meant to touch.

It swirls and it curves,
well on its way,
showing me which way to go,
on this bright, sunny day.

Splash of Ink

She was a black, splash of ink
on a white, crisp vase
She stood loud and proud
and made no mistakes!

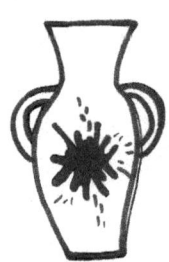

She Is

She is the Earth,
in her nurturing way—
softly moist and nourishing,
capable of growing life,
but fiercely witty enough
to create landslides—
don't be caught in the friction.

Le silence de la nuit

perdu dans le silence de la nuit
cri de pleurs entendu à l'infinie
tellement loin, aigu et distant
était le son de mes larmes
tiré du creux de mon âme

incognito, que j'aimerais tellement être
si loin d'ici, au loin de cette fenêtre
d'où je cherche constamment, pour un monde différent
de celui où je vis maintenant

amour oublié, chatouillement de ma peau
quand tu es près de moi, viens me retrouver
si distant, dans le silence de la nuit
depuis plusieurs jours je t'attends

Dont You Cry for Me

There are no tears in heaven.
So, dont you cry for me—
I'm drinking beer and laughing
with my brothers next to me.

My mother, I have finally seen
so many years of sorrow—
it seems to be bittersweet
without you two, so hollow.

don't shed any more tears;
I cannot wipe them away.
The years will pass and so will time;
the pain will fade away.

I am not an angel.
It is nothing but a lie—
if guardian angels are so real,
why am I here tonight?

I know you have lots of regrets.
Believe me, so do I.
The things I'd change if I returned
would be a great accomplishment.

Beneath the clouds, I clearly see
all who have judged me.
I don't care; I laugh at thee,
the many lies only I can see.

I have waited four long years.
No white horse has appeared.
Mom, brothers, dad, and friends,
you're up there, drinking beer.

Oh my, how she misses you …
She hopes for the day
she will see you.
Soon—no, for she is here with me,
the soothing voice of sincerity.

Grasp Into Nothingness

I could almost grasp her hand,
but through the thick fog
I was unable to see
that it was, indeed, a mirror—
and that reflection belonged to me.

Wicked

Follow me into the darkness.
There, something grim possesses
the inner darkness
that surrounds the light,
not letting it shine through.

It is wicked,
like the dancing flames
in the campfire.
Promises of beauty and fear
dancing all at once,
all as one.

Fire's Glowing Light

Oh, I have had many nights,
sitting by the fire's light.
I can see into the bright.

The sudden and warm firelight
has me believing that
everything's going to be alright.

Your body is my most appreciated sight;
take me out into the night,
let's leave our worries for another time.

I'm loving my time with you.
Do not fight the feelings,
let them shine through.

They can be the nightlight
when I walk down
this dark path, with you.

Let me be your guide;
may luck be on your side—
your beauty truly is sublime.

And if I die tonight,
I can tell him that I've met my match
and that I can fly.

I have never seen true beauty,
til I saw her here tonight,
by the fire's glowing light.

Promise of Forever

When I step out onto this dance floor
on this beautiful night,
lullabies and reminiscences of an older time
(your beating heart and that sweet, sweet smile)
the promise of forever, as I hold you tight.

A Tear

Today, a tear has been shed
as I lie weary in my bed,
with thoughts of a better time
rolling rapidly throughout my mind.

The saltiness on my tongue
from the pouring eyes above,
leaves a streak of emotions, so …
showing the tears which way to go.

Paint Me a Picture

Paint me a picture,
full of color and strokes.
Create for me a masterpiece,
of wonder and hope.
Help me imagine
a new world, just for me;
imagine a life
where my paintbrush's creations
become reality.

Connection

Unable to see the greatness in it all:
unproductive, like an unplugged wire.
No connection, nothing fires.

Nap Time

Nap time, nap time,
it's a fun time.
Close your little eyes,
let me sing you a lullaby.
Night night, little child,
dream of angels
as I hold you tight.

Beauté à l'infinie

le soleil, la nuit, le tonnerre et la vie
les étoiles scintillantes, les sons de la pluie
gouttes, diamants à l'infini

My Darling

I'll pray for you my darling,
for your soul to be at rest.
You were the greatest blessing;
you were nothing but the best.
May all your dreams be vivid,
may they be so full of life.
You were nothing but shining stars
on a dark and solemn night.

Hey Dad

Hey Dad, how are you?
I turned thirty-one today
and I wonder the things you'd say
and all the things we'd talk about …
if you were here.

Were you there, as I walked down the aisle
to marry my best friend?
Tonight, I raise my glass to you.
I am me and you're still you …
and all my dreams have come true.

Hey Dad, I hope you're okay;
I hope your stress and pain have faded away.
One day we'll have a glass, or two,
and catch up on all that's new …
I know, we miss you, too.

Can you see who I am
and what I've become?
Are you proud of me?
Oh oh oh oh …
Do you see me kiss my children goodnight
and hold them tight?
Oh oh oh oh …

Wax

Candle wax, leaking slowly …
Warming up the skin,
exciting the senses.

Barbers Bay

The waves are crashing
rhythmically on the shore.
The waves stretch
as far as the eyes can see,
where they then, disappear.
In the distant fog,
tall birch leaves
fall to the ground,
one after the other,
as if taking turns
jumping down.
Then, the yellow mosaic of leaves
patch the green grass;
the wind blows the yellow leaves
down into the water—
where the waves are dancing,
and the ducks swim by.

Forever Smile

The breeze felt so nice on her body.
The smell of the air made her smile.
The beauty in the sky
and the crickets saying goodnight,
birds singing a sweet lullaby,
made her forever feel alive.

I Looked For You

I looked for you in the darkness—
where I was scared, alone, and lost.
I could hear your voice echoing
through the thick and gloomy fog.
I tried so hard to find the door
that kept our worlds apart.
From the start to the end,
from the end to the start,
I roamed around til I heard you,
begging me to stay.
I followed your voice,
the sweet escape
that helped me find my way,
away from the darkness
of these halls.
Away from the light
that shone so bright
and back to your arms,
where I belong.

Flower Crown

Build me a crown of flowers,
for it is full of beauty and life.
For in the presence of its glory
my soul will quickly come alive.

He Says

He says walking is running slow,
and I'm not sure which way to go.
I'm swaying in every direction—
if I run, I'm falling fast.
I fear I will not last.

I think I've come to a conclusion at last,
that everything will be fine.
It just takes a little time
to find out who you're
going to be.

You will fall,
and you may fail;
you will leave a busy trail.
With persistence, you will prevail.

The nights will be long;
with daylight comes a little song.
Melodies inspire my journey.

So long, my only friend.
Thanks for telling me that I can;
I'll never give up, yes I can.

I see the warmth of your eyes
brightening up my lovely life.
Make me smile the rest of my life.
Make me smile the rest of my life.

Emotional Fluctuations

My Mother Lips

I cry when I am worried.
I cry for what is not,
but I worry every single day
and get those very painful thoughts …

that one day, you might not be there.
That one day, we'll be apart.
Oh, please don't do that
to my tender and gentle,
fragile heart.

I whisper to you softly
and kiss you when you sleep.
Your forehead's warmth
on my mother lips,
makes warm, my rosy cheeks.

You fill my heart with rhythm
and my mind so full of stress.
I long for peace of land and mind
and make sense of all the rest.

Solitude

dans ma solitude
j'apprends à me connaitre
et à m'aimer

The Last String

When the last string has been strung
and the last song has been sung,
let the melody fill your ears.
May you have no more fears.

Father

I dreamt about him once.
He was on a rooftop made of pebbles,
a window with bars divided us.
A barrier from my world, to his.
His chemise was a seafoam green;
he puffed on his cigarette, once
before putting it out.
He gave me a reassuring smile,
as if to say that he was at peace,
that he was okay, and that we would
see each other again, one day.

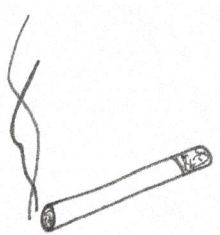

Promise of Tomorrow

At night, the sky, before the dark
layers of blue to green
dim out into yellow,
then fade out into orange and pink:
the promise of tomorrow isn't sure
but the beauty in its arrival
is certain.

Capture a Moment

I'd like to capture this moment—
Your smirk, your cheeky smile.
I want to remember this moment—
before we say goodbye.

Face of Glass

She has a smile painted on her face, of glass.
You cannot see which emotions lie beneath this mask.
She can paint a smile, some lips, or a grin,
it is seemingly so profound.
Underneath, she permanently frowns.

Grasping Reality

I need to grasp reality.
You're not coming back to me.
I wish I could have helped you;
it simply wasn't up to me.
It was out of my hands,
that is the reality.

The Heat

In my hands I hold the heat,
letting go will burn my feet.
Holding on will make me weep.

Ink

The black ink, dark as tar
fills out the blankness,
empties the mind.

Ton visage

cette journée-là
quand tu n'étais plus là
j'ai dit au revoir
à tout espoir

et le beau temps
était parti
pour toujours
à l'infini

je me revois
dans cette maison
jour après jour
comme une vision

et puis l'image
de ton visage
semble si loin
mais reste sage

Hold My Hand

Catch my soul as it rises,
hold it tightly in your hands.
Get a grip of the emotions
that we are both feeling,
as we lie here, hand-in-hand.

Hold my hand til I'm gone,
til I live only in your heart,
til I glow only in the warmth,
til I'm seen only in the light.
Our memories linger in your mind.

Forever's a long time to be alone.
Please be happy, do not frown.
You can never let me down.

The Deserving Regret

It seemed you saw how great she was,
when she had finally had enough and left.
She was finally roaming free;
you were left there, with regret.

Nature

Nature
gives me literal air
when I figuratively can't breathe.
It gives my brain peace,
it takes the scattered pieces
and distributes them to the earth.
Then, the thoughts fill the cracks and the holes,
repairing them and liberating the mind
from such haste.

Vanilla Skin

Warm vanilla skin,
kisses on the neck
with thick, juicy lips.

Trapped in Despair

Do not ask him about nature.
Do not ask him how crisp is the air,
for he is not worthy, he is not prepared.
He sits down in the darkness,
he doesn't breathe in the air;
he's trapped inside himself.
He does not care about your air,
for he cannot breathe
the crisp, summer air.
He's trapped in despair.

The Field

The field of yellow stretched
as far as my eyes could see—
blue skies and cotton candy clouds
illuminated our journey.

Crisp, summer smells filled the air—
daisies and wild flowers
we picked to give to her,
as a token of our love.

The possibilities were endless!
Our imaginations flew as free
as the bugs who had wings;
they ... could go anywhere.

We played and laughed
and hid in that field.
The sun said good morning
and the moon tucked us in.
Then, we lay in the grass
and stared at the stars.

The Strokes

It is not the brand of paint
that makes the artist—
it is the talent in which lies the hand
that makes the strokes.

Emotional Fluctuations

Scrub it Away

Scrub my pain away,
make it bubble up and pop.
Wipe the memories off the floor,
rid the walls of all their thoughts.
Scratch the worries out by layers,
tell the cracks to sort things out.
The more I scrub, the less I feel.
Forgetting all the thoughts.

Ma mère me dit

ma mère me dit
je ne te changerais pas, pour tout l'or du monde
et j'espère bien qu'après ma mort
que tu t'aimes, autant que je t'ai aimée
je t'aurais donné le monde entier
ne te laisse pas marcher dessus
je sais que tu as un grand cœur
ne te stresse pas avec les choses
qui sont hors de ton contrôle
vis bien dans le présent
serre fort tes enfants
tu possèdes mes valeurs
la couleur de mes yeux
je veillerai sur toi
comme les nuages autour de moi
confortables et accueillants
comme les bras de ma mère
depuis plusieurs jours elle m'attend

Aurella

She was born
on a cold winter day,
in a time where people
lived the simple way.
She walked, twenty-five inches tall,
short, fierce, and full of smiles,
locks of smooth, curly hair
and a fire in her eyes.

She was a hardworking woman.
Throughout her years,
never stopped, never slowed down,
or got old.
She had the eyes of innocence
and a heart of gold,
the sweet smile of an angel
and a sense of humour, so bold.

She was an inspiration
to be the best that you can be.
If I could be
even half the person she was,
I'd be very happy.

Stéphanie Bouchard

Country Air

Out there, I am fair.
I am without a care,
in the crisp, country air.

Sudden Bliss

I can breathe in the air
that comes forth from your lips,
as you whisper, *I love you*.
Then, from one gentle kiss
comes that tingling feeling,
sending me to sudden bliss.

Picking Up My Pieces

I'm picking up my pieces;
I'm scattered on the floor.
I want to be the person
that I once was, before.
I'm shattered pretty good this time;
it's much worse than I'm letting on
but I'll shove it deep,
where my stomach lies,
til the people are all gone.
Then, I'll put away my smile
(like a shirt tucked neatly in its drawer)
and think of the memories
of who I was, before—
before my pieces
were scattered on this floor.

The Plank

She gazed upon a wooden plank
and followed it to the end
where it led her to the riverbank—
tis a path to freedom's land.

Antisocial

I am a triangle in a world of ovals.
We do not fit together—
sometimes I try but my edges stick out.
The corners are sharp,
in a soft, squishy centre.
Different worlds come together—
then, apart.

OCD

Place the soap on the left.
Scrub that stain once again.
Check the stove.
Close that light.
It'll take me a while to say goodnight …

Close the door.
Check the lock.
Make sure the kids are breathing.
Spray those germs, they are dying.

Wash my hands til they are bloody.
Wish I could talk to somebody …
feet are much too messy,
I don't know where they've been.

Scrub again, take a shower.
Full of germs, no more laughter.
Don't do that! That way,
someone's going to die.
Count and organize.
One more time.

Souvenirs d'enfance

cette odeur dans l'air frais
me rappelle mon enfance
où j'ai passé mon temps à courir
dans l'herbe fraîchement coupée
qui me chatouillait les petits pieds

Blinding Light

The dimming of the light
was nothing but a lie—
for those who experienced death,
saw but a bright and blinding light.

Sultry Kisses

Falling onto you,
lying hand-in-hand.
Lipstick kisses show where I've been,
sultry kisses in the sand.
Promises of tomorrow,
whispered softly in my ear.
With you the world seems fine;
everything seems so clear.
You linger in my mind,
as good as a picture.
If I had one wish on Earth,
I would keep you, a little longer.
When my mind turns to dust,
oh, the pieces may shatter,
memories fading in the distance,
out of reach.
When I see his eyes, I smile.
Holding me close as I cry,
I wonder who's this lovely man,
showing me a picture of us,
hand-in-hand.

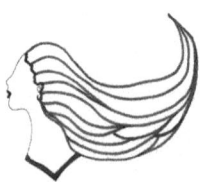

Emotional Fluctuations

Raindrop

It came from the clouds,
then it dropped on its head—
it changed the lives of everyone
but not itself.

I fear, for in time
it will not be able to see
that once it falls to quench the earth,
its wellbeing does not come first.

My First Love

Lay me down in a field of daisies,
where I am brightly illuminated.
By the day's fantasy,
touch me softly.
Follow the curves
that form my body.
The grass and your smile
are the day's scenery.
Held forever, deeply,
in my warm, beating heart
is the never-ending memory
of my first love.
Love forever binds us,
even when we are apart.

The Wall

I'm staring at the wall.
It still hurts but
I'm okay with the pain.
Okay with it all.

I'm looking straight ahead
but seeing far beyond.
Sitting on the edge,
finding the point of it all.

Sensitive Heart

I'm sorry that I didn't speak up
when it was the time,
that I took the blame
for things I didn't do,
that I didn't speak up
when I should have.
That I was the dirt
underneath your shoe.

I'm sorry that you misunderstood
and thought my politeness was flirtation
and that I was too shy to speak my mind,
no matter what the season.
I'm sorry that I lingered and wasted
so much time …

Emotional Fluctuations

My heart was too big, sometimes,
and sensitive hearts do hurt,
for every foul word
is a prickly stab
on an organ full of hurt.
Let this be a lesson,
to those who easily scar.
Let only those worthy of your love
into your fragile and brittle heart.

The Trees

I look for inspiration in the trees—
the way the branches dance
so effortlessly in the breeze.

But even they, so independent and free,
without reason
were constrained—controlled
by the seasons.

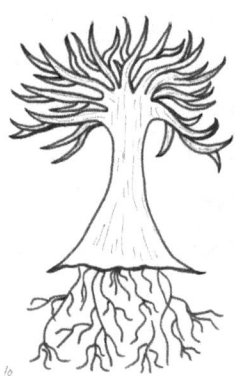

Sister and Brother

(For: Alex and Isabelle)

Come, little sister …
Come, play with me outside,
in the hot summer sun.
Let's run and hide!

Let the sun's rays
bounce off your copper hair,
let it warm our souls
and show promise of hope and possibility.

Okay, brother …
please show me the way.
Let imagination lead the way,
on this hot summer day!

Pure Winter Air

Breathe in that pure winter air,
inhale the pureness of the wind.
Feel the snowflakes melt on your skin,
gaze upon their beauty and yours, within.

Calming Heart

So, I close my eyes
and take a deep breath …
Slowly breathing,
calming the heart.
Dreading the day
we'd both be apart.

Stéphanie Bouchard

My Saddened Face

I look into my tired eyes and saddened face
and think that through my tears the feelings are erased,
permanently effaced.

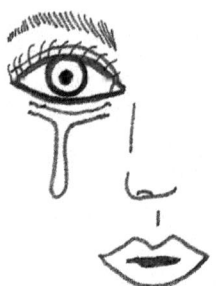

Cup of Tea

Pour me a cup of tea.
Let me feel its warmth
upon my hands and cheeks.
Let me tell you about my day,
about my worries and fears.
I need a fresh mind's advice,
a change in atmosphere.

Yo-Yo Mind

My mind's a yo-yo of emotions—
up and down, always in motion
—forever in the day's moment.

Highway

Mustard yellow lines
stretch, as far as my eyes can see.
Cloudy skies and the reminiscence of memories,
followed by a sweet, summer breeze.

Stéphanie Bouchard

A Patch of Frost

A patch of frost amidst the branches
creates a mosaic of colours
on all the leaves, big or small.

Onto Me

Fall onto me,
let your hands drop into mine.
Hold me close,
til our bodies are entwined.

She Feels of Blue

She feels of blue
and bleeds of red,
cries in black,
she's filled with dread.
A shade, a hue,
she feels so blue.

Let Me

Let me be merry and bright
on this magical night.
Let me be grateful for my life
til my last goodnight.
Let me hold you tight
by the fire glow's light.
Let me give you a gift
of endless love and laughter.
Let me be your love.
Let me be your forever.

Freaky Fiction

A box has arrived.
Its contents are unknown.
As I open up the sides to look,
I open my mouth to groan—
for when I open up the box so big,
its contents are filled with bones.

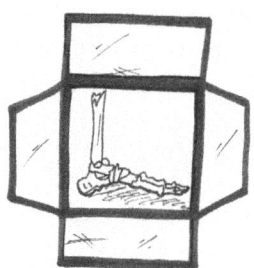

Routine

Routine is what keeps the busy mind
and the body's soul, at rest.
For they need consistency and care
to make sense of all the rest.

This Floor

I'm not looking for any trouble
while I'm dancing on this floor,
I'm just looking for a place to jump,
to wiggle away my sorrows,
from the night before.

I'm not looking for any trouble
when I'm shooting down
my shots like water,
It quenches my thirst
and washes away the thoughts
that commit inner
and outer disasters.

Elements

(For my uncles)

I am still here.
I am not far.
I still live in the middle of your heart.
I've crossed over to the other side.
I've dreaded the day we'd say goodbye …
I am still here.
I am the air.
I know my absence is unfair …
I am still here.
I am the earth.
The sickness and regrets came first …
I am still here.
I am the water.
Don't worry,
I remember only the laughter …
I am still here.
I am the fire.
Holding you in my arms,
is my heart's desire …

Fiery Skies

Starburst and fiery skies,
painting the night in orange.
Lead me into the night,
lightning in the sky.

The rain, the nighttime's lullaby
rushing in without warning;
lean back, cover your eyes.
Luminous sight.

Thunder shockwaves in the sky,
brightening up my life;
nature's beauty paints the night.
Illuminate my eyes.

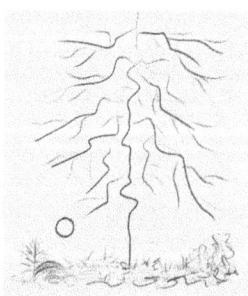

The Blackness Paints

The blackness paints the darkest of souls
and leaves where there used to be light,
a dark and empty hole.

Blurred Line

My hot breath on the mirror
creates a blur between vanity and reality.
In its apparition I can write
the words I chose to live by.
I stare into the blueness of my eyes
and find inner and outer beauty,
which then takes me to the place of acceptance
where I love myself, no matter what.

Passionate

Castle of Blue

There's a little white house in the country,
in this small northern town,
with fields of hay and wildflowers,
where imagination runs free.

There she stood in the doorway,
there to greet me with her curly grey hair.
Eyes of blue, like the ocean,
I wish I could go back there.

But out she went for a little adventure,
she left this place of green.
For the castle of blue,
she flew high and never looked back.
Her life was written in joy and harmony;
I know she'll miss me,
I will miss her equally.

I'm jealous of the bright stars.
They are much closer to you;
they illuminate my journey.
I hope all your dreams come true ...

Love you dearly

I will guard your heart
and protect all that is you.
I will protect you from the dangers of the world
and make your days happy.
When mine are not,
I will kiss your forehead
before you fall asleep.
I will answer millions of questions a day
because you need to know all of the answers,
I will love you endlessly.
Hold you closely.
And love you dearly.

Wintery night

I feel alive
on this wintery night,
surrounded by shimmering lights,
whilst the spirit
of forgiveness is alive.

Emotional Fluctuations

The Me You Don't Know

The me you don't know keeps everything inside
and holds you a little closer,
when you're sleeping, at night.

Repetition

Every day is repetition.
Daily tasks are repeating.
My mind is deadening.

Suffering inside my box of thoughts:
in here—it is frantic and fast,

days fly by, one faster than the next.
Organize. Arrange. Plan.
I'm in a daze …

Every day the stress grows,
it overwhelms and grips my mind.

every day is repetition.

Show Me

Show me the drive
that pulls you towards goals,
that takes you away from the bottom,
and from the ashes, rises you to the top.
With no intent to stop,
show me the faith you have in yourself.
When all else fails
and you lose your beliefs,
including your way.
Show me the drive
that'll bring you to a better place.
I hope courage
will show its face.

Tattoo

My body absorbs the ink
much faster than you think.
My body tells a story.
It is like a picture book,
take a closer look.

Joy in the Little Things

I find joy in the little things,
amazed by the details.

When it rains, you stay inside and hide,
shielding yourself from the showers.

I bask in its refreshing gift
and splash around earth's residue.

I breathe in the fresh summer breeze
and smell the fragrance of nature's collection
and its bright coloured wildflowers.
I, find joy in the little things

Rare Find

Sometimes people have
their minds made up about you,
without even knowing you
and that's just fine.
You are too perfect to share;
I am glad you're only mine.
What a rare find!

Fear

It grips me,
takes me by surprise.
Tells me I'm not good enough
and takes away my willingness to try.

It stops me on my way,
scares my soul,
and changes the way I think;
makes my heart beat
too fast.

It hurts to think.
Scrambles my thoughts
and makes everything
so complicated,
it exaggerates the details.

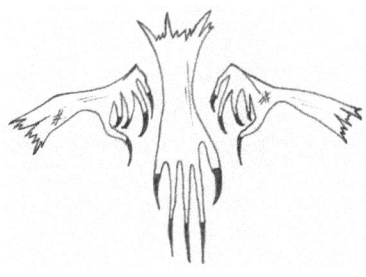

Field of Acceptance

I'll meet you in the field of acceptance—
there, everyone is accepted.
Come, when the sun's about to set,
it sprinkles the land with beauty.

There, you will smile and feel loved
by the day's embrace, with warmed cheeks
from the setting sun.
Then, maybe you will love yourself.
I … always have.

Emotions of the Day

May we not judge a person's actions and words in a short matter,
for it is the emotions of the day, spewed out in an hour.

Stéphanie Bouchard

I Came from the Earth

I came from the earth and grew with the trees;
I moved like the flowers, swaying with the breeze.
I saw the top of the Earth as I flew with the bees.

Emotional Fluctuations

The Bite

Flickering lights,
making shadows on the wall.
Afterwards, there was the ice.
The cold was felt first,
later, came the bite.

The Abyss

My eyes' tears blend in with the shower water's warmth.
The eyes, a blank stare, wander off, afar, to the past.
A clear sign of depression.
The metal swirls of the shower head
become a lined blur,
the tears are then dragged away
by a tourbillon, into the abyss.
A black hole sucks the emotions
and leaves a clean slate.

The Pieces

I once was shattered into pieces,
a puzzle too hard to match.
As I picked the ones I thought I should,
I got rid of all the rest at last.
I kept the pieces that I needed, though.
They are keeping me intact.

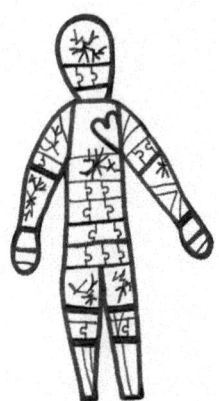

From Scratch

I made you from scratch.
I made up all that you are
like a recipe, nothing but the best.
Pieces of me, pieces of him
made the loveliest creation.

These Trees

These trees take a stand
and invade the land.
Sleeping in their sheets of cold
until the permanent heat
rises again.

Miles Apart

I carry you with me always.
In my soul, within my heart,
even when we are miles apart.

Inner Ghosts

I'm sorry that I wasn't there
when you needed me the most.
I wish I could have saved you
from the haunting recurrences
of your inner ghosts

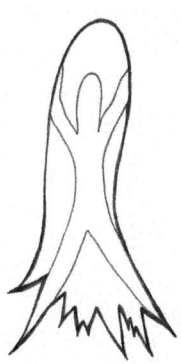

I Aspire

I aspire to be something great.
I am full of dreams and hope.
I can see potential in myself,
and I can imagine what will be.

I am proud of what I am.
I remember what has been
and think of what is to come.

Speck of Turquoise

A speck of turquoise on a sheet of white,
keeping account of the space surrounding it.
Being consumed by blankness—
the combination of all colours.

Fireflies

Fireflies are the stars
of the Earth, not sky,
showing a path of light
on a dark and gloomy night.

I'm Falling

I'm falling off the edge …
I'm dangling …
I'm stepping off the ledge … I'm dying.

I'm dying … off goes a light.
I'm thinking …
I'm gone with the wind …
A whisper.

A whisper … a softly spoken phrase.
I'm missed but not forgotten …
It's over but everything remains the same.
I've simply passed away my pain …

Stéphanie Bouchard

Creativity

The people who didn't have much money,
they were the most creative
because they made the best of what they had.

Swirls

Spirals of undecided colours,
not sure which way to swirl …
unaware of their surroundings,
life's simply just a whirl.

Stéphanie Bouchard

It Comes Down Like Glitter

It comes down like glitter.
Twirling round and round,
pushed by the powdery wind,
it shimmers with a mesmerizing glow.
Then, it falls beneath, onto the diamonds,
on this cold, beautiful wonder
called snow.

Emotional Fluctuations

Endless Love

Love me today,
on to the next.
Vow to love me
endlessly, til the end.

Semicolon

People will miss you;
please do not leave this world.
Right now, you're a mess;
your opinions may differ.
You feel only mental pain,
like there's nothing left to gain.
But it'll get better with time,
if your heart can bind.
Give your thoughts time
to turn around;
you can't change your life
for the better …
if you're in the ground.

The Quietness of it All

The quietness is unbearable …
In the quiet of it all,
I can hear my thoughts and feel emotions;
they are the loudest sound of all.

Photography

With this device I can capture a moment:
here, time stands still.

On this piece of glossy paper, your smile is permanent;
what a thrill!

To see your true self, so sublime:
here, you hold me in your arms,
til the end of time.

Like Diamonds

The snow shimmers like diamonds.
It reflects light from the sun.
She says, *it cannot be so,*
there's magic in this stretch of snow!
It sparkles for a while,
til it ends in the darkness—
there, it stops abruptly.

Then, the magic returns in an instant
to a spot where the sun is so bright,
leaving her in wonder—
this magical thing called snow.

Her Body

Her body was as gentle as a petal;
she smelled of sweet lilies and fresh rain.

Her hair swung back and forth
like the salty ocean waves.

Her eyes, a lapis of blues,
like the sky and all its glory

vigorously pumped blood
throughout my vessels.

The Dark

The dark swept over the world
like a finely placed sheet.
The darkness covered the sun
in a swift motion.

Like the wave of a hand,
it was done.

People forced to live in the abyss
of what their world had come to,
an abrupt end—
the result of peoples' inadequacy.

Stéphanie Bouchard

Pendulum

When my eyes are closed,
my mind's a pendulum of thoughts.
The phrases forgotten by day,
come out at night to linger and play ...

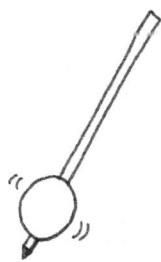

The Cracks

So, we drove there in silence,
as the dust settled down.
The wind blows away every memory
that I've ever known.

From the ashes, I've risen.
From every spark grows a light,
but the sadness I've been feeling
has yet to arise, tonight.

Waves of emotions
travel my spine,
but in the arms of my loved ones,
I have found the light.

When the glass has been shattered
and glued back a million times again,
its mosaic of pieces and colours.
Makes all of us wonder—
all seems stable but you can always see the cracks.

Stéphanie Bouchard

Clever Rain

The rain is so subtly clever,
without ever knowing so.
It washes away my sadness—
the rain is nature's trickery;
my tears are invisible.

Honey Coloured Eyes

My soul was the gloomy dark of night,
til, in the honey-coloured eyes of a man
(just like the scorching and cozy sun)
I found bright and warming light.

Stéphanie Bouchard

The Dangers

Follow me into the darkness …
Here, the dangers are grave,
but we cannot see them.

Life Hasn't Been

Life hasn't always been easy.
Life hasn't always been fair.
I've found myself at the bottom;
I've found myself in despair.
Life hasn't been forgiving.
Life has been overbearing.

But I ... have been resilient

Music Box

Inside this object,
music is held.
It is a song keeper.
When you open it
(after cranking it)
the graceful ballerina
twirls on her nimble feet,
while dancing to
A ballet music beat.

Seasons

Fresh crisp leaves
and tall autumn trees.

Newly cut grass
and an afternoon breeze.

Spring showers
grow these beautiful flowers.

Snowflakes like treasure.
Please, just one more hour …

A Million Reasons

I can think of a million reasons
why I love you so.
many things left to say
before I let you go

Mistake

This mistake burns deep;
it haunts me.
It keeps my heart twisted in knots

and my mind racing,
trying to imagine its reversal.

If not this,
differences in possibilities would arise

I would be different;
my mind would be at ease.

My heart wouldn't hurt,
and my cheeks would be dry.

Look Around

Let's make the best of every day;
each moment is filled with joy.
Let's cherish all the little things;
my heart is filled with love.

Do not forget to look around
and feel the wind upon your cheek;
let the flowers grow wild
and the grass tickle your feet.

No Peace

No peace can stay upon this earth;
it's washed away with all its worth.
They take a stand, decorated in dirt,
to free the world of all its hurt.

The Wind

The coldness of the wind came first.
Afterwards, came the glacial rain.
It took them away from the outside world,
luring them in,
forcing them to spend time with family
which took away their pain.

Dance with Your Hair Down

Wear your hair down tonight;
we are going dancing …
Wear your finest dress,
with heels so high;
I'll take you out dancing
into the night.
The wind on your cheek
will make you feel alive;
you make me smile.

Wear your lips of red
and shadows of gold;
you make me feel
so well and bold.

We are going dancing …
I will twirl you around and around,
You will never touch the ground;
in my arms you're safe and sound.

I have loved you every day,
since we first met.
The days go by so slowly when we feel alive,
so wear your hair down tonight.

Monsters

There are no black holes here.
No sorts of what they say—
the underworld is an empty landscape;
the devils have gone to play.
But aren't there any terrors,
lurking so deep underwater?

I cannot remember
the last time I saw any horror.
For here, you'll find some worth;
there are no monsters here—
they are all roaming the Earth.

Working Hard

Work hard, till there is nothing left;
it's almost over, take a deep breath.
Mindfulness is key;
forget the rest.

Something Nice

Her soul is like a block of ice—
please, tell her something nice.
His heart is like a raging fire—
tales and lies, a pumping disaster.

Unconditional Love

Hold me forever, hold me tight.
Your hands are my escape,
your voice, my lullaby.
In your eyes, I see my future.
In your heart, unconditional love lies.

I Lost Myself

I lost myself in the branches.
I lost myself in the depths;
I lost myself in the darkness,
where I was truly overwhelmed.

I found myself in the grass.
I found myself in the light,
where I was enlightened by the glow,
its positive radiance,
like shimmering lights in the snow.

How You Grow

Stop thinking about what you said or did,
many years ago.
Mistakes are how you learn,
they are how you grow.

Blaze

Fall into the blaze of life and get burned—
then, come out strong and wise
from the fiery life lessons
you have learned.

Hand in Hand, Side by Side

Walk with me, hand in hand,
until the sun rises again.
Sleep beside me, side by side,
til the moon tells us goodnight.

Goodbye, sweet lullaby,
until tomorrow, where we'll meet again.
Where, in your eyes,
I'll find my love, my best friend.

The Reaper

There will come a time
where the time will pass away,
so fast you won't believe.
The reaper will come to please.
Life and death are one,
like the planets and the sun.

Self-Acceptance

It didn't happen all at once.
It took many years to come true;
I am still fighting for it now.
Sometimes I long for self-acceptance;
some days, I'm already there.
I've loved myself from the very start
but some days I am unfair—
unfair to my body, to my courage,
and my world.
If I can love myself on a daily basis,
in myself, I'll find some worth.

Emotional Fluctuations

Continuous

I'm up and out,
out and about,
about and ready,
ready to go out,
out into nature.
Nature is so relaxing,
relaxing are the times.

Stéphanie Bouchard

Gazing Eyes

My eyes were gazing
into the dark.
We were a million miles apart
but it is in times like these,
(when loneliness steals the part)
where we find out who we really are.

Rise Again

I am hidden
behind this wall of pain;
I cannot break down.

The sunshine
will rise again,
when hope is found.

Forgive Them

Forgive people for their foolish ways,
for they are the ones
who will fight an inner battle,
for the rest of their days.

Tape Your Ticker

Do not ask for tape to patch your ticker
from the one who broke your heart,
for you will be left with a mess
that is much worse than the start.

I Cannot

I cannot do this …
I cannot fight.
I am too tired …
let's say goodnight,
until tomorrow,
where I can make sense
of all the things
that cause such sorrow.

Emotional Fluctuations

How Long

I walked the line
A hundred times.
I've seen the day
where you said
goodbye.

How long
will you be gone?
To save us from self-destruction …

When will I see your face?
When will I see some improvement?

Blankness

An emptiness, a blankness,
a fresh-written page.
A world of endless possibilities,
a brand new stage.

Emotional Fluctuations

Broken

She had owned a piece of his heart,
since they were young.
Together,
the pieces made a whole.
When he left, it was as if that piece
was replaced with rock—
the weight weighed down her heart,
and the tears filled out the rest.

Stéphanie Bouchard

I Called For You

I called for you in the dark—
you didn't hear me.
I called for you in the light—
you didn't see me.

The Clock

The clock ticks to show the time;
its ticking is consistent.
It does the same job,
day in and day out,
and wants to be a person—
a person on vacation
—where time is out of the question.
Where we care not about numbers,
no schedules, or routines.
Like people, not machines.
Oh, it feels so great to dream …

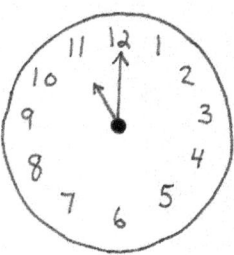

Stéphanie Bouchard

Warmth to the Bodies

My aura is as bright as the sun—
rays of positivity
shine through my skin,
sharing my warmth with bodies
who are cold and depressed—
bringing them to life.

The Path

Follow the road, it'll show you which way to go.
Follow the path, you'll come to a conclusion at last.

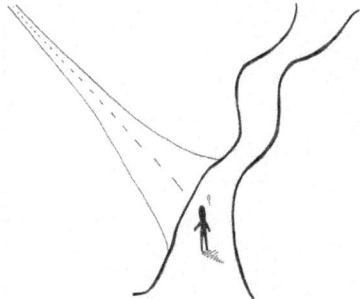

Stéphanie Bouchard

Glitter on the Floor

Picking up remnants of glitter on the floor,
from the magical night before …
I love this man with all of my heart.
Like the glitter in the cracks,
may we never part.

I Cry a Pond of Sadness

I cry a pond and swim inside
and splash around its sadness,
to get out wet and drag around
droplets of regret,
which I then sprinkle on the ground,
so it can wear a coat of sorrow,
just until tomorrow,
where there I start again.

Bottles

Picking up bottles,
clinkedy-clank,
gathering them up as I clean.

They are empty now.
They used to be full,
their insides a liquid,
they used to hold.

Its contents when ingested
change a personality so,
or make an honest person bold.

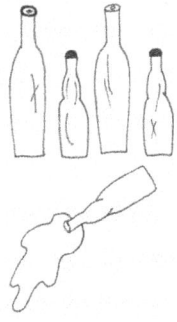

Don't Leave Me Here

Please, don't leave me here, alone.
I've fallen down to the ground;
I've fallen and I can't get up …
please, take the time to pick me up.

A Block

It's a block, stop!
An unclear mind,
some useless thoughts …
not sure what to write.
The words aren't coming out right!
It's a wall so big and tall
that blocks the words from coming out at all.

Heart of Lead

She had a paper thin heart,
it was fragile from the start.
He had a heart of lead
and weighed down hers,
to avoid the shreds.

Stéphanie Bouchard

I Wonder

I wonder what they think about,
when they're lying in their beds …
Are they dreaming of cotton candy clouds?
Having visions of dancing teddies
in their heads?

Are there lollipops instead of trees?
Are the flowers made out of bubbles?
Is there a rainbow in the sky each day?
Are there never any troubles?

As they skip along the way,
may the cuddles of a million angels
protect them each day,
til the morning's gleaming glow arises,
where they will then happily
march confidently on their way.

Shattered Pieces

Shattered pieces of a heart,
put back together, like a jigsaw puzzle.
Mended, till all that's seen are the cracks …

Sleep

Hold me in your comfy arms,
take me into a sudden and abrupt daze
where I can escape reality.
Each night I come to you trusting,
with open arms and closed eyes.
I long for rest, fulfill my need to sleep
with the ritual that clears everything
and starts fresh in the morning.

She Smiled

The coldness of her hands made me shiver.
Was she okay, I wondered?
She smiled, but through her teeth.
She dared not speak
and spent much too many days worrying.
She was not well,
lost in repetition.
In her eyes I saw no vision.
A broken down woman
with lovely eyes,
a mixture of three colours, or more.
But inside there was no hope,
nothing left but a blank stare.

Alcohol

Let me take my gin
and wash my sorrows within.
Let me take my vodka
and tell you how I want ya.
Let me take my whisky
and get a little frisky.
Let me take my liqueur
and become a vivid dreamer.
Let me take my rye
and think too much and cry.

Black Cat

Black, black
dark as night.
Don't step on cracks …
Black cat,
hissing, with its lifted back.
Mad, mad
broken glass.
Curiosity killed the cat …

Ivy

Kiss me with your deadly kiss,
surround me with green.
Wrap my neck with orange hair
and make me do things
I cannot control.
Command me,
touch me quickly;
I am not immune to toxins.
Temptress, we have become one.

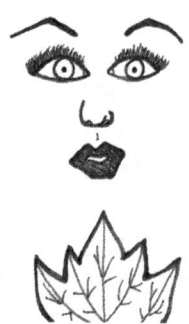

Ramore

This small town
is filled with
hermits, nature lovers,
homebodies, and beer drinkers.
Here, not much changes but the weather.
It is tranquil and beautiful,
nature at its finest.
Here, you grow old;
you make memories
and build families.

Silver Tree

Silver tree with
crimson leaves,
glowing bright.
Up on the tree,
shining bright.
Equally scattered,
pretty reddish leaves,
their color swaying
in the autumn breeze.

Golden Flakes

There was something about the painted golden flakes
that created a classic beauty—
gold trim on black.
Inside the granite,
little specks of golden flakes
brought beauty and life
into the dull rocks,
creating everlasting beauty.

Luminous Being

I think you are beautiful luminosity,
the way you shimmer
even when you are surrounded by darkness.

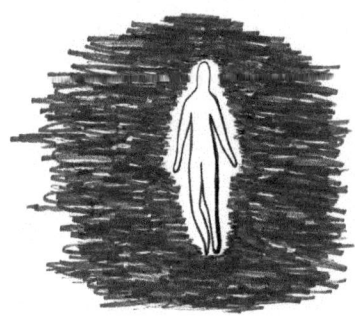

I Gave You All

I painted the stars in the sky for you …
you stared at the ground.
I created the oceans' water for you …
you sat in the sand.
I made the most beautiful bed of roses …
you slept in hay.
I gave you all;
you gave nothing back.

Chocolate Canvas

His brushes left specific streaks
and planned out traces.
Up and down the soft, sleek, wavy canvas,
leaving prints of where they've been.
Dragging chocolate across this erotic map,
untouched, unexplored.
He started from the top
and made his way to the bottom,
painting from side to side,
concentrating on certain areas
longer than others,
til it was all a chocolate blur.
Reminiscences of an older time
went through his mind,
from when he was an artist.
It was similar in many ways,
except the canvas was her body,
and the brushes were his fingers.

Flower in a Patch of Weed

Why did you never try to understand her?
She was a flower in a patch of weeds.
A beautiful, chaotic mess
who's ripping apart at the seams.
In her, you must believe.
You must leave her time to heal ...

My Rainbow's Bright

Why do you cast a shadow over my rainbow
and put darkness on my bright.
Let me shine all of my colours,
near and far and out of sight.

Never fill me with doubt again.
I have potential and greatness
that makes their way
through all of the darkness,

revealing nothing but light,
no matter the inner fight.
I will be ok.
I will be alright.

Emotional Fluctuations

The End

In the end,
I will have nothing left to do
but hold your hand.

Stéphanie Bouchard

Trapped Under Water

She's trapped under the water …
I need to get her out;
I need to take a stand
and let her out on land.

She wiggles and she's blurry
and doesn't seem to mind,
for why is she not afraid,
she's been there for some time …

I started screaming loudly,
but no one was around.
I jumped in, it was quite the fall,
I was so afraid to drown …

I couldn't find her in the waves;
she was constantly in motion.
She reached out her hand to help me get out;
I had jumped in for her reflection …

Emotional Fluctuations

Up Here I Wait

Up here, there is no pain.
Just the sorrow of missing you so,
and the constant promise of tomorrow ...

The Setting Sun

Will he visit my grave?
On a cold and rainy day,
to whimper at my resting place,
his hair dripping from the rain.
Will he see the setting sun?
With memories of me
rolling through his mind,
smiling at the clouds up above;
a tear rolling down his cheek,
holding his children
in a warm and tight embrace.
Will he lay down roses?
Where I eagerly wait …

Tea Party

Tea,
tea for you and me.
Let's sit together,
dressed up at our best—
my jet black hat
with a paisley sash
and your pretty chiffon dress.

Inextinguishable Spark

You were the one who let me down easy
and caught me each time I fell.
You gave me the push I needed
when I was truly overwhelmed.

You are the light so bright
that shines through all my dark;
you are the flame, the fire,
the inextinguishable spark.

The Changes

When the sun shines above the sky,
when the moon greets me
to say goodnight—
green glow in the sky,
fireflies …

When the rain drops on the ground,
puddles, water, all around,
safe and sound—
but all alone
in my home …

Sometimes we are not so brave,
left to be wowed, to be amazed—
Spooky stuff amazes us;
we decorate without a fuss …

Stéphanie Bouchard

Cold and shivery are the days
we all go out of our way,
smiles and surprises all around—
the chirping birds are all gone,
not a sound …

The Slowness of Honey

The saltiness of his tears
leaked out of his eyes
with the slowness of honey
dripping into the sea
til he was surrounded
by its salty misery.

Stéphanie Bouchard

You Are Poetry

You, in this light,
is what poetry was invented for.
You are poetry in motion.
You are it, in the flesh;
you exude.

www.ingramcontent.com/pod-product-compliance
Ingram Content Group UK Ltd.
Pitfield, Milton Keynes, MK11 3LW, UK
UKHW022214230426
12048UKWH00016BA/841